Other Issues in
The Jon & Jayne Doe Series

ISSUE #1

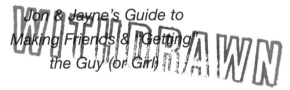

*Jon & Jayne's Guide to
Making Friends & "Getting"
the Guy (or Girl)*

Stay Tuned for These
Upcoming Issues

ISSUE #3

*Jon & Jayne's Guide to
Getting Through School
(Mostly Intact)*

ISSUE #4

*Jon & Jayne's Guide to
Teen "Flings" ('n Other
Guy/Girl Things)*

Hey, Justin.
Thanks for the inspiration!

Jon & Jayne

Jon & Jayne's Guide to Throwing, Going to, and "Surviving" Parties

You're Invited!

To: Issue #2

When: Right now

Where: Inside

Till: As long as it takes

RSVP: ☑ COMING
☐ NOT COMING

HCI TEENS

Health Communications, Inc.
Deerfield Beach, Florida

www.hcibooks.com

The authors believe the information and advice presented in this book are sound and relevant. However, it is recommended that you seek the help of a certified professional if you are facing serious challenges in your life. This book is not intended as a substitute for consulting with a professional mental-healthcare practitioner.

The term "hookup" as used in this book refers to hanging out with someone you like and making your feelings known.

The pseudonym "Jon and Jayne Doe" represents a creative and qualified collective of teens and adults. All characters in this book are fictitious unless listed as one of the crew (see pages 115–118).

The Library of Congress Cataloging in Publication Data is available through the Library of Congress.

ISBN-13: 978-0-7573-0726-3 • ISBN-10: 0-7573-0726-4

Printed in the United States of America.

Publisher: Health Communications, Inc.
      3201 S.W. 15th Street
      Deerfield Beach, FL 33442–8190

"Dr. Toni," Pico, and Iago caricatures by Larissa Hise Henoch
Cover design and interior design by Carol and Gary Rosenberg

PASSWORD: |⬚⬚⬚⬚⬚⬚⬚⬚⬚⬚⬚⬚⬚⬚|

This book is your password to throwing
excellent, memorable parties and
getting involved w/ others to
celebrate life and good times.

It's also the key to something new & fun,
a different way to share your world.

If you forget your password,
the hint is . . . *Jon & Jayne*.

FUN

WHAT'S INSIDE...

FEATURING STORIES FROM:

- Alex
- Alina
- Ashley
- Carlla
- Danny
- Jacob
- Justin
- Krista
- Max
- Skylar
- Wilson

Hey! Welcome to Issue #2! In case you weren't here for Issue #1, we're Jon Doe & Jayne Doe (no relation, just good friends). We represent **people like you** who want to be heard **LOUD & CLEAR.**

We live in a world of 7Fs—friends, fun, fights, family, feelings, fashion, and flirting. It's probably a lot like your world. We have **concerns** about the future (another "F"!) and about getting by in school (no "F" for that) and in social **situations.** It's not always **easy,** and sometimes it's really tough. But we all seem to get **thru it** somehow.

** **W**elcome to **O**ur **W**orld*

We want to know what you—and people like you —have to say. Sharing our **feelings** on different subjects can help us make sense out of this **7F world**.

Things like how to throw a **good** party, how to be a good **guest**, how to avoid poor **choices**, and how to help out seem so **basic**, but these are **important** things to consider for creating good memories we'll have **forever**.

We've got a lot to say on the topic of **partying** . . . and we bet you do too!

Be Heard. Be Yourself.

JONANDJAYNE.COM

LOG ON TO OUR WEBSITE, WWW.JONANDJAYNE.COM, AND JOIN THE 7F COMMUNITY. POST CONUNDRUMS, SHARE STORIES, TELL THE WORLD, TAKE THE SURVEYS, GET ANSWERS TO THE QUICKIES, SOLVE THE DRAMA, AND MORE. SEE U THERE & IN HERE!

cHaT_

JD GaTEr 110:   r u goin 2 felicia's party 2moro nite?

JaynE SaYs 611: idk seems kinda last minute u?

JD GaTEr 110:   heard its gonna be awesome ....she invited everybody

JaynE SaYs 611: seems a little too much

JD GaTEr 110:   her parents r out of town

JaynE SaYs 611: ...oh

JD GaTEr 110:   thats y she's having it

JaynE SaYs 611: maybe goin isnt such a gr8 idea

JD GaTEr 110:   come on u have to go!

JaynE SaYs 611: do not

JD GaTEr 110: but everyones gonna b there

JaynE SaYs 611: i just dont think its a good idea

JD GaTEr 110: y

JaynE SaYs 611: i hardly know her... who knows what'll happen

JD GaTEr 110: come on it'll be ok

JaynE SaYs 611: omg just forget it

JD GaTEr 110: fine i'll let u no how it is ....so what r u gonna do instead?

JaynE SaYs 611: i was thinking about callin this guy I met at the mall....

JD GaTEr 110: hmmm... oh whatevr.... have fun w/ whoever he is...

JaynE SaYs 611: hah, Jon, r u jealous?

JD GaTEr 110: yah, rite

JaynE SaYs 611: nite jon

JD GaTEr 110 has signed off.
JaynE SaYs 611 has signed off.

What's your story?

THE SCENARIOS

Where do you fit in?

Got something to celebrate? Whether it's your birthday, a holiday, or some xtraordinary achievement, what better way to celebrate than by having a party? We've got some great ideas to share w/ you for throwing an amazing one!

Graduating? Whether it's to a new school or just the next grade, the end of the school year just **SHOUTS** "Party!" You know it and you wanna get ready to have a blast!

No invite? That's okay. You can learn how to throw a party of your own and build your group of friends at the same time. It doesn't have to be a huge bash. Start small and set yourself up for more fun in your life, if that's what you're looking for.

Just wanna have fun? Yeah, well, that's what parties are all about. Whether you throw them or go to them, it's all about having fun and making social connections. Unfortunately, parties aren't always fun and games. But we'll try to help you keep it that way. It just takes a little common sense.

Are you on the party-planning crew? Throwing a party can be lots of work, so if a friend of yours is having a party, find out how you can help and write down the ideas you read here and ones you come up with. Then share these ideas with your friend and help him or her organize an unforgettable time!

got a good party idea? post it in the 7F forum on jonandjayne.com

Don't wanna wear out your welcome? Don't blame you. Find out what makes a great guest who's sure to be invited back. And while you're at it, why not find out what makes a great host. The best way to get invited back to parties is to have parties of your own.

Last party got out of hand, huh? You're looking for safe, but fun, ways to entertain your guests. It's easy and it's all here in this issue. Take our word for it, things really don't have to get out of hand for your party to be memorable. It's just better that way for everybody.

Just curious? OK, so you just wanna read a good book and get to know what we're all about. Well, you came to the right place!

■ ■ ■ ■ ■

In this **issue**, you'll find 5 keywords. You'll need these to unlock the **clues** to the **Drama**.

How will you know when you find a keyword? **Easy.** We'll say something like, "So, the keyword here is _____." Couldn't make it much easier than that!

When you find a keyword, go to jonandjayne. com, click on "Oh, the Drama" and follow the instructions. Each keyword unlocks a clue. Solve the drama in as few clues as possible.

GOOD LUCK!

Oh, the Drama!

Our friends Andy and Claudine hooked up in bio last semester, and they've been dating for 3 months. Everything was just "perfect" till (in a crazy fit of xtreme honesty), Andy told Claudine that if a certain celeb asked him for a date, he'd take her up on it! What kind of insane thing is that to tell your girlfriend?!

So, who is she? Claudine wants to know. Help her figure it out. And we will just say, "Andy, there's such a thing as being too honest!" Try this keyword: "Moderation."

Parties are a great excuse to let go and have a good time. Simple enough, right? But we all know that nothing's really simple (except for *really* **simple** things). All kinds of stuff can happen at parties—most good, but some not so good, and maybe even pretty **bad**. You can definitely set up for **success** and avoid disaster (in most cases) if you use your head and **BYOB***.

The **ultimate** goal of a party is for everyone to have fun, right? **No doubt** about it! There are lots of ways to have a great time w/o going over the edge. If you're throwing a party, the first order of **business** will probably be who you're gonna invite.

---

* That's "Bring Your Own Brain," not booze.

Sometimes making up the guest list can be the **toughest** part of planning a party. Are you having a big party or a small get together w/ a few friends? Think about how much **space** you have and **definitely** don't invite more people than you can fit. **Remember, it's a party, not a mosh pit.** Once you know about how many people you're going to invite, begin to make a **list**.

You'll want your **bffs** to be there, but what about the people outside your immediate **group**? Think about the **guys** & **girls** you'd like to get to know better, and take a **chance** by inviting them too.

Start by keeping a list of the **"yesses"**—people you plan to invite. Keeping a "no" list is not a **good idea**. What if the list ends up in the wrong **inbox**? There may be lots of hurt feelings.

We avoid inviting people who have a **bad rep** for going overboard or making **trouble** at parties. If you're taking people off your list for this reason, **be sure** you aren't simply depending on **rumors** for your info. If someone's a **trouble-maker**, you probably know it firsthand.

Next thing you need to consider is, are you gonna send out invites or do it by **word-of-mouth**? When making this decision, keep in mind that a word-of-mouth party can easily turn into a huge disaster. **Ahhh!** You invited 15 people but 51 show up (and no more than that if you're **lucky**). If you wanna keep things under **control**, sending out invitations is the way to go. That's why "**invitations**" is the keyword. Too late for this **advice**? That's ok, go to page 61, Oh No, Pandemonium!*

So now the last Q is, do you hand deliver the invites or mail them? **Think** about it. We've seen people get into really big **fights** when someone hands out invitations in front of peo-

ple who aren't **invited**. If there's enough time, we think **mailing** the invitations is a better idea.

Last-minute parties are something else. You won't have enough time to mail out invitations and get your guests to **rsvp**, but a guest list is still important. Tell anyone you decide to invite **NOT** to "spread the word" about your **big party**.

Plan your guest list carefully or you may end up with a party that spirals out of control, down into the **perilous** pit of *PARTY PANDEMONIUM!*

COOL WORD—LOOK IT UP.

SkyLar'S tory

Issuing the Invites

Choosing who to invite to your party has a major impact on how fun the event will be. Inviting some people and not others can cause drama, but it's a party, so there will be drama no matter what. To keep the drama to a minimum, I always make sure my closest friends are cool with the people I plan to invite. We go through the yearbook and discuss the different people. If we all agree, I'll add them to my list. I never invite anyone I don't know.

It isn't important to me to have the most popular kids in school at my party. Yeah, I could invite the hottest guy in school to impress everyone even though I barely know him, but I'd be in a bad situation when he shows up with all his buddies and makes my party a disaster.

I recently sent out invitations for my Sweet 16, which is coming up soon. I followed my own advice, and I'm psyched for what I know is going to be an excellent night. When people at school heard I was having a party, some of them were more friendly because they wanted to be invited too. But I know from experience to watch out for the users. That never works out well for anyone.

I'm happy with the guest list I ended up with. I plan to have a list at the front door so if someone shows up who's not on the list, they can't just crash it. My parents would not be into that and neither would I. A lot of careful planning went into my party guest list, so I know it's gonna be hot.

Skylar H.

Skylar's party *was* totally hot! We had an excellent night, dancing and eating. All the guests were cool and no one caused a bad scene. She was right, though. There was some drama, but it was a mellow drama and it blew over pretty quickly. We're so glad we made the guest list, cause she's very picky. Thanks for the xtraordinary time, Skylar!

AsHLey'S
tory

The Spectacular Disaster

I was so excited when I got invited to what was supposed to be the most amazing party. A lot of people were on the guest list. It was being held at the biggest, nicest place I'd ever been to. I mean, it was *three* stories with outrageous decorations. There were so many people there. I knew a lot of them from school, and I was expecting to have a great time hanging out with them.

On the first level, there was a huge board for the guests to sign—the kind that has a picture of the guest of honor on it. Guests were signing it all over like they were supposed to with funny sayings or mushy sentiments and stuff. But when no one was looking, these mean kids graffittied the board and wrote really nasty things all over it.

The parents who were hosting the party gathered all the guests who were under 21 in one room and basically yelled at them. It was really uncomfortable for all of us—especially for the people who didn't even do it. The party went downhill from there. *Goodbye, awesome night.*

So it turns out that it didn't matter how great the place was or how amazing the food and decorations were. What ended up mattering was that some of the guests ruined the whole thing for everybody.

Ashley B.

As the saying goes, "The party you throw is only as good as the people you throw out of it." Ok, we made that up—it's not a real saying, but we think it gets our point across . . . or maybe not. Whatever. What we're trying to say is that just a couple of idiots can ruin a good time for everyone. Invite only people you know & trust, even it it means fewer guests.

JUSTIN'S Story

Thank God
for My Friends

I was looking forward to the party I was going to have for my Bar Mitzvah, and I was really careful with who I was going to invite. I made sure that everyone on the list was someone I considered (or my parents considered) a friend (or relative). Still, getting ready for my Bar Mitzvah was a drag. Every week I had to go to my rabbi's house and study everything that had to do with Judaism. I knew it was important, but it was a lot of work. So I kept looking on the bright side: the party.

The day started with the services. To help calm my nerves, I kept thinking, *As soon as the party kicks on, it will be a blast.* That's what made me keep pushing to succeed. The faster I finished the services, the faster the party would start. As soon as I was done, I felt like a huge weight was lifted off my back. I couldn't believe it was over and done with—successfully!

When the party started, people were just sitting around and talking. I was waiting to make my entrance, but I looked in and saw that not much was going on. I was worried that all the effort would be for nothing.

Thank God my friends were there. As soon as the music started, they got up to dance. The DJ announced my parents, then my sister, then they made the biggest entrance for me. All the guests out on the dance floor clapping and shouting, all just for me. I felt great.

The food was amazing—the cake was even better, especially because I cut it right down the middle with a samurai sword that I got when I'd earned my black belt. Everything that could have gone right did, and it turned out to be an extraordinary party. I know it doesn't always work that way, but when you have the right group of people (and some money from your parents), it usually goes pretty well.

Justin O.

Sounds like Justin's bar mitzvah celebration was a success. Religious milestones, like bar/bat mitzvahs, Confirmations, etc., are always great reasons to throw a party.

The religious significance of these events is usually a personal matter, so we won't even go into that, but whatever the case may be, tradition usually equals celebration. And who better to party with than friends and family? Justin got that part right.

As far as $ goes, parties usually require some. It's great if our parents can cover the expenses, but not everyone has that luxury. Fortunately, parties can be fun even on a tight budget. After all, when it comes to a great party, it's the guests who matter most.

Not on the "VIP" List?

When there are big things going on like milestone **celebrations** (confirmations, bar & bat mitzvahs, graduations, sweet sixteens, and **stuff** like that), it seems like there's a **party** every weekend. We know it can be really **uncomfortable** when it seems like everyone around you is **talking** about a party you weren't **invited** to.

The good news is you aren't the only one! Feeling **left out** is something most of us face at one time or another.

If you're like "**never**" invited to parties, chances are you don't have a very big group of **friends**. That's ok, but did you read **Issue #1**? If not, check it out. It's got some good **ideas** for getting to know people. Meanwhile, here's a way to grow your social **party circle** (if you want to):

1 Start by planning a small party of your own. Invite the friends you have, even if it's just a couple of people.

2 Find the courage to invite a couple of acquaintances and ask your friends to do the same. If each of you invites two people, you'll have a good-size group.

3 Use some of our ideas for throwing a party and your guests should have a good time. If they do, then, those people are more likely to have you at a party they're throwing.

Don't worry that there's something **wrong** with you if you don't turn out to be a big party-goer—even if you "**try everything**" to get yourself invited. Remember, there's something to be said for "trying **too hard**." Try not to be too **pushy**.

Ahhh! It can get sooo complicated sometimes. In fact, "**complicated**" is the keyword. Not everyone can be supersocial and absolutely **no one** can be **everything** to **everybody**. It's not even worth trying.

WiLSON'S

story

Belonging

I don't usually get invited to parties and when I do, I don't feel like I belong at it. Instead of feeling bummed out about not going to someone's party, just throw one yourself. Sure feels a lot better than not being invited to one. All you really need to do is have some friends over that you can have a good time with, some food and drinks, and something entertaining to do.

You don't need to give in to peer pressure, like smoking or drinking. Those are two of the stupidest things I think a person can do—especially when you're young. They can really mess up your body and your head.

One day, I was with my cousin and we had nothing to do that night so we decided to have a party of our own. We called our friends and told them to come over. It wasn't a really big party. There were about twelve people. We played video games, watched movies, played mahjong, and just talked and hung out. It was an unforgettable night for me, because it was the first time I actually felt like I belonged at a party.

Wilson P.

It's not the end of the world if you don't get an invite. There's always something else to do. And if going to a party means getting involved in stuff you don't like just to fit in, you're better off not going.

Wilson's right that you and some close friends can make your own "party" by just hanging out together and doing something fun. It doesn't have to be planned beforehand or be big and fancy. Just a few people spending time eating, drinking, and having a good time. That's our definition of a party anyway.

ALiNa'S

story

Left Out?

About a year ago, there was going to be a party, and half my grade was invited. I was one of the people who wasn't. When I asked my friends to hang out that night, they told me they were going to Derek's party. Derek was a boy I had dated, and it didn't end smoothly. I quickly changed the topic so my friends wouldn't ask me if I was invited.

That Friday night I stayed home and hung out with my family. It wasn't so bad. The next morning my friend called and told me the party was a total dud. It was so noisy that the neighbors called the police and two police cars came and three kids got arrested for bringing a hookah (a big water pipe) to the house. Also, one of our friend's boyfriends was caught upstairs with another girl.

At school that Monday, a lot of people said they regretted going to the party. After hearing that, I was glad I didn't get invited!

Alina B.

Sometimes getting left out of something turns out not to be such a bad thing! (Think about all the disastrous parties we weren't invited to. *Whew!*)

Alina and Derek clearly weren't on speaking terms, so really, why would he have invited her to his party? We can't expect to be invited to parties given by people we aren't friends with.

If some of our friends are invited and we aren't, that's when it gets sticky. If they decide to go, we shouldn't hold it against them. And it doesn't seem like Alina did. That's cool.

A good PARTY thrower . . .

- plans for a party in advance
- has a guest list and sticks to it
- plans fun stuff to do at the party
- has enough food and drinks to go around
- makes sure the party is safe and sets boundaries
- mingles with all of the guests, even with people on the outskirts
- doesn't get all stressed if things don't go exactly as planned

A good party GOER . . .

- shows up on time
- brings a gift if it's that kind of party
- doesn't cause problems or start fights
- tries to help out by tossing garbage and stuff
- treats the other person's property with respect
- joins in whatever the party-thrower has planned
- mingles w/ the other guests, crosses cliques
- doesn't monopolize the conversation
- knows that when the party's over, it's over (Go home!)

WHO SAID IT'S FASHIONABLE TO BE LATE?

We think it's **kinda rude** (unless you told the party-thrower you'd be late beforehand). Try to be on time (or no more than a **1/2 hour** after the party's supposed to begin).

There was a guy named Joe Hardy.
Who was always up for a party.
But he'd always be late.
And make everyone wait.
So we said don't come if you're tardy.

That's cute, Jon.
Did u make that up
yourself?

Yeah, it's a limerick.
u like it?

Uh-huh

Go to
JONANDJAYNE.COM.
CLICK ON "CONTESTS" AND
ENTER YOUR OWN LIMERICK FOR
A CHANCE TO BE IN THE
SPOTLIGHT!

Hand Over the Mic!

Seems like our friend Mike *always* has to be the **center** of **attention**, especially at parties where he's in *ppm* (perpetual performance mode). He can top any **story**—even if he has to make it up or make it sound **better** than it really was.

Sometimes it seems like he's only **listening** to what other people say so he can chime in with **something** he thinks is more **important** or exciting. Yeah, he can be lots of fun, but sometimes we wanna say, "**Chill out**, Mikey!"

There are lots of people like Mike who raise their **voices** above everyone else's, **thinking** that what they have to **say** is more important or entertaining. We **ALL** have things we want to share, and we think the Mikes of the **world** need to hand over the mic to someone **else** sometimes.

There's nothing wrong w/ wanting attention and entertaining people, but if you have a *captive* audience instead of a *captivated* one, you might want to step over and share the spotlight.

Spotlight on Mike

I was born to be an entertainer! I plan to be an actor or maybe a comedian someday, or both! I am a funny guy, really. Sometimes it seems like I'm just making things up, but crazy stuff happens around me all the time.

Of course I want people to like me, doesn't everyone? If I think there's someone in the group who doesn't like me, I guess I try even harder. Maybe too hard sometimes.

To be honest, I really like the attention! It makes me feel good. And I also like to make people feel good. I guess I should try not to hog the spotlight all the time. But, hey, I've gotta be myself, don't I?

We love you, Mike!

Mike makes a good point. We did say "be yourself," didn't we?

Celebrate.

Celebrate.

Celebrate the good times

In this **mixed-up** world where it seems like there are so many things to be **sad** about, it's really **important** for us to take time out to celebrate the things in life that we think are good. Sometimes it might seem like the **world** is falling apart, but if we look hard enough, we can usually dig up some **good** stuff.

The good things don't have to be **monumental** events. They can be as **simple** as the first hot day of the **year** or getting a pet or a new bike or a new bf/gf, or even passing a **test** or a class by the skin of your **teeth***.

*Do teeth have skin?

Oh, JON, you are so literal!

Celebrations don't have to be huge **blowouts.** Just a friend or two can help you celebrate whatever you think is **important.** You can do small things to celebrate, like bake some chocolate-chip **cookies** from scratch, see a movie you've been wanting to see, whatever. Or you can even go all out and throw a **party** to celebrate. The choice is yours. . . . It usually is. Remember that keyword: "**choice.**"

The more you praise and celebrate your life, the more there is in life to celebrate.
—Oprah Winfrey (you know her, right?)

Spring is nature's way of saying, "Let's party!"
—Robin Williams, a funny guy

Tip ☀ 2

Choose your music carefully and have a good variety.

Tip ☀ 1

Set the mood by adjusting the lighting.

Tip ☀ 3

Put up decorations for holiday or theme parties.

Tip ☀ 4

Put away breakables and valuables in a safe place.

Tip ☀ 5

Arrange furniture to make room for dancing.

Tip ☀ 6

Have some extra seats available like folding or stacking chairs.

Setup & Layout

There's a **reason** they call it "party planning." You've gotta have a **plan** if you want your guests to have a good time. Like we said, start with your guest **list**. Once you get that down, start making a list of all the stuff you'll need.

Here's what our party planner, Mindy (see page 118), says are the things that are most important (food and drink are another story):

35

- Short, clear plastic cups (3 per guest min.)
- Paper plates (3 per guest min.)
- Forks, knives, and spoons (2 of each per guest min.)
- Serving bowls for snacks
- Lots of cocktail and regular napkins (and paper towels for spills)
- A table for food (with cool tablecloth)
- Straws and drink decorations (like paper umbrellas and plastic swords)
- A table or counter space "bar" for drinks
- A table for games or gifts
- At least one great, fast-paced board game
- I-pod or CDs with good music

Cross these items off your list as you get them. (BTW, you can probably borrow some of this stuff.) Whatever you do, don't wait til the last minute to get it together. Running around before the party is a real drag. You'll have other important things to do to prepare for the great time you're gonna show your friends!

J&J

MINDY'S GOT SOME GREAT RECIPES FOR MIXED DRINKS AND APPETIZERS. GO TO "THE 'NO-BOOZE' BAR" (PAGE 47) AND "TEAZERS & FILLERS" (PAGE 51).

Got Game?

Let's face it. Formal party games went out with **goofy** hats, **creepy** clowns, and leaky balloon **animals**. So, when we talk about games, we're not talkin' about pin-the-tail-on-the-jack---er, **donkey**. You may not need to have games at your **party**, but it's good to plan something just in case things begin to border on **B-O-R-I-N-G**.

If you have a **dart board**, pool table, air hockey, or table tennis, you can hold **matches**. But this is usually more **fun** for the people playing than the people watching. Same goes for video games. If you're having just a few people at your party, this may be the way to go. Board **games** get more people involved, but any game you play should be **fast-paced** and be able to include lots of players.

Games like **Make Me Laugh** where you do silly stuff and players "try" not to laugh can usually get everyone laughing, and scavenger hunts (when you have the space) can also be really fun. **Theme** parties, like murder mysteries, are a bit involved, but it's still cool to get into **character**. (Small groups are best for that type of game.)

Of course, Truth or Dare, **Spin the Bottle**, and similar games are always gonna show up at some party **somewhere**. And some people are always gonna be up for them. But keep in **mind** that those games may make some of the people at your party **uncomfortable**. No one should be pushed to play if they don't want to—don't **force** anyone to do anything they don't want do. Also keep in mind that **kissing** random people can be even grosser than **double-dipping**. And if two people are "together," it might create some awkwardness, even **jealousy**. Consider this scenario:

66Once I was at a party w/ this guy I was totally crushin on and I just knew we were going to hook up. But then everyone wanted to play Spin the Bottle. So this girl in the circle got to kiss my guy and they ended up exchanging cell numbers. I was crushed alright.**99**

—Cali

Kissing games may also catch you **off guard**, and kissing is really something you wanna do when (and if) you're **ready**. This is a bit **gross**, but listen to what this guy Jeffrey has to say:

"It was getting late and everyone was sweaty and tired of dancing, so someone suggested we play 7 Minutes in Heaven. I got picked to go into this really tight closet with this girl I liked. When I reached out to put my arms around her, I got a whiff of really skanky body odor—it was me! The dancing lasted longer than my deodorant. She shot out of that closet in under a minute. It was really embarrassing.**"**

—Jeffrey

Wanna get close w/o being too **obvious**? Play the classic party game *Twister*. (Don't forget deodorant!) This game has been around for almost forty years and it's still pretty **cool**. Some things don't go out of style.

So anyway, whether or not you have games at your **party** is your call. But like we said, have **something** planned as a backup. But don't worry if it turns out that no one's **into it**.

M a x ' s t o r y

Why There Are Parties

I'm not quite sure why "the party" was invented, but I have an inkling. I think parties are an excuse to chug Pepsi and have video game marathons. And sometimes, it's the best way to really love being an idiot.

I've been playing a video game that simulates guitar playing (called Guitar Hero) for a while, and recently, another one came out—Rock Band. This one was designed for four people, one simulating singing, the guitar, the bass, and the drums. It's the perfect way for four friends to look like morons and enjoy themselves at the same time. So, after saving my allowance for three months, Rock Band was sitting in my room. It was time.

Time to make my guest list, anyway. I flipped through my phone's saved numbers. After passing up several people who either didn't play the game or were too dignified, I found Aaron and Dylan, two good friends of mine. Physically, they're almost polar opposites—Dylan is big and Aaron is light, but they get along well, probably in mutual craziness. After Jack fell through, I called Bryan, an old friend from elementary school—and it was complete.

Bryan showed up first. He was a Guitar Hero veteran, so he moved to the drums and learned them. Then came Aaron, who, after learning the drums, picked up a guitar. Dylan got to my house last and almost got forced into the lead singer position, but I took mercy and decided this was an opportunity to embrace my destiny as the next Ozzy Osbourne.

After setting up the game, we tried out "Dani California," by the Red Hot Chili Peppers. The song itself didn't actually go so well, especially because Aaron tried to play the guitar solo with his teeth and my rock star poses turned out better than my singing. And both me and Bryan missed half the song because he threw a drumstick at me. And then the Pepsi and Oreos came out, which made us do great on the first few and then not so good. And the caffeine factor took down most of the band around 1:00.

But the moral of the story—and the good news— was that we all acted like total idiots and had a great time. And that's *truly* why there are parties.

Max V.

See, you don't need a big crowd to call it a party. Just a couple of fun-loving friends, a great game, "good" music, and some simple snacks will do it. You can totally plan a small get-together around some cool game or activity like Max did. And you can get to act like an idiot, too!

Idiot's a good keyword, don't ya think, Jon?

Nah, Let's wait for one that doesn't hit so close to home.

What's more fun than **planning** a surprise party?! Well, we *could* name a few things . . . but it's still on the list of **fun** things to do! Part of the fun of throwing a surprise party is keeping it **under wraps** (we have some tips 4 that), but you also should try to avoid **scenarios** like this one:

> ❝It seemed like every time I turned around, my friends were talking behind my back. I knew they were getting together sometimes w/o inviting me. It just seemed like they were keeping secrets, and I felt really bad about it. I'd ask them what was up and they'd just give me that innocent look like nothing's going on, but I knew something was.❞

How can you avoid making the person you want to make feel special feel unspecial? This way:

#1 Do your planning on your phone when the guest of honor isn't around.

#2 Make an agreement not to talk about it at all if there's any chance the guest of honor is suddenly going to appear and surprise you to the point where you make up some stupid story or just completely fall silent, followed by a really awkward moment.

#3 Assign tasks to different members of the "party-planning crew" so you don't all have to go out together to shop and make arrangements and leave the guest of honor out in the cold when he or she would normally be w/ all of you.

How to Plan a Successful Surprise

☑ Set a date and make sure the surprisee is going to be available. Call his/her parents to let them know what you're planning so they don't make any last-minute family plans.

☑ Come up w/ a believable activity that you, the guest of honor, and a couple of friends are going to do the day or night of the party.

☑ Organize a "party-planning crew" and give tasks to each person, like get the supplies for the drinks/food, make this or that recipe, and so on.

☑ Send out invitations at least 4 weeks before the party. Make sure everyone who gets an invitation knows it's a surprise.

☑ The time to arrive on the invite should be about 45 mins before the surprisee is expected. Remind people not to be late—they could blow the surprise. (Joe Hardy, you're not invited.)

☑ Act like you normally would when you're w/ the surprisee. It can be hard to keep a secret, especially when you're all excited, but you've gone thru this much trouble, so stay cool.

☑ Come up w/ a believable way to get the surprisee into the party. If it's in your house, you can pretend you left your sneakers or flip-flops in the den (or wherever the party is). Think about it. You'll come up with something.

☑ Shout, "Surprise!" (Duh.)

Subtlety

Be Yourself!

That's one of our favorite things to say (and it's one of our favorite things to be!*). Since the effects of drugs and alcohol can cause us to do stuff and say things we'd never do or say if we were straight, it totally goes against the "Be Yourself" philosophy. (Go check out Dr. Toni's Spine-Tingling Truth on page 81.)

*It's also the title of our theme song!

See our video at jonandjayne.com

The No-Booze Bar

Our party planner, Mindy, helped us come up with these excellent crew-approved, **zero-proof** party drinks. (Thanks, Mindy!) She says you totally don't need alcohol to make **fabulous** mixed drinks, and she's so right! They look awesome, taste great, and are **fun** to make and serve.

If you have some extra cash, forget the boring plastic cups and buy some cool, reusable plastic martini- and margarita-style glasses. Why not? The drink doesn't have to be alcoholic to get dressed up! (For smaller parties, your parents might even let you use the glass ones.)

alcohol-free "MyTini"

● ● ● Jon's Jack 'n' blue ● ● ●

1 1/4 cups frozen blueberries

1 1/2 cups lemon-lime soda

1/3 cup of sugar

Splash of lemon juice

4 plastic swords

16 fresh blueberries

Combine frozen berries, soda, sugar, and juice in an electric blender. Whizz it up till it's real smooth. Pour into four short glasses. Spear four fresh blueberries in a stack with plastic sword and drop into each glass as a garnish. Serve w/ a short straw.

● ● ● Jayne's Pinky colada ● ● ●

2 tablespoons heavy cream

2 tablespoons cream of coconut

2 tablespoons of grenadine

8 ounces of pineapple juice

2 cups crushed ice

4 maraschino cherries

4 pineapple chunks

4 plastic swords

Combine heavy cream, coconut cream, grenadine, and juice in your electric blender. Whizz it up really fast. Pour into four short glasses. Spear pineapple chunk and cherry with sword and drop into each glass as a garnish.

DON'T FORGET TO add a CUTE UMbRELLA! —JaYNE

Hey, Jayne's drink may LOOK "girly" but it tastes GREAT!! —Jon

● ● ● Wavebender ● ● ●

12 ounces gingerale

4 ounces orange juice

Grenadine for splashing

4 slices of orange

1 ounce lemon juice

Fill a shaker halfway w/ ice. Pour all of the ingredients (except grenadine and orange slices) into the shaker. Shake very gently, then strain into four martini-style glasses. Add a splash grenadine to each drink and lay an orange slice on top.

← That's a shaker, by the way.

Duh!

● ● ● Mytini ● ● ●

8 ounces passion-fruit juice

2 ounces cranberry juice

2 splashes lemon juice

8 maraschino cherries

4 plastic swords

Lemon-lime soda, for splashing

Fill a shaker halfway w/ ice. Pour all of the ingredients (except the plastic swords and cherries) into the shaker. Shake well. Strain into four martini-style glasses. Top with a splash of soda. Spear a cherry or two with plastic sword and drop into each drink.

Have some soda, juice, and bottled water on hand for anyone looking for a "softer" drink.

● ● ● Krewzoosky ● ● ●

8 ounces orange soda

8 ounces orange juice

4 ounces lemon-lime soda

Whipped cream

Grenadine for splashing

Fill four short glasses with ice. Pour an even amount of orange soda into each glass. Then do the same with the juice, then with the lemon-lime soda. Put a small scoop of whipped cream in the center, then pour a splash of grenadine over the whipped cream.

● ● ● The Black Hole ● ● ●

24 ounces of grape drink

8 ounces of orange juice

Purple grapes (no seeds!)

Pour grape juice and orange juice into a big pitcher and stir. Pour into four short glasses filled with ice. Drop a couple of grapes into each glass and serve cold.

Party drinks don't need alcohol to taste good. Your grocer may have non-alcoholic frozen drink mixes in the freezer section. It's a quick and easy way to have frozen "mixed drinks" at your party without having to mix them yourself.

Hey Jayne,
Wat is THAT?

It's an old-fashioned freezer.

Teazers & Fillers

Gonna have a party? Gotta have **FOOD** (that's a big "F"). You can start with the basics like chips, pretzels, and other snacks like that. But it's also fun to prepare some **cool dishes** of your own. Our party planner, Mindy, helped us come up with these pretty easy-to-make but **xtraordinary** recipes.

● ● ● Skinny-Dippers ● ● ●

8 ounces sour cream

1 packet dip mix

Empty sour cream and dip mix into a large bowl. Stir well. Chill for a couple of hours. Transfer to 2 festive serving bowls. Serve with baby carrots, cucumber sticks, and other sliced veggies on the side.

● ● ● Great Guacamole ● ● ●

1 package of frozen guacamole

1 bag o' tortilla chips

What's great about this recipe is that you don't have to mash the avocados. Defrost the sealed package of guaca-mole in the fridge (if you're in a rush, soak it in a bowl of warm water). When soft, transfer to a serving dish. You can add chopped fresh cilantro, onions, tomatoes, and a few dashes of hot sauce. Garnish with a sour cream blob and sliced black olives.

LA SALSA

Pour one jar of hot, medium, or mild salsa into a ceramic serving dish. Couldn't be easier!

● ● ● Hades' Hummus ● ● ●

1 package of plain hummus

4 large pitas

1/8 cup olive oil

1 teaspoon chili oil

1 teaspoon cayenne pepper

Toast pita bread in a toaster oven to make it crispy. Cut each pita into 8 even triangles. Scoop hummus into a serving bowl. Pour in olive oil and chili oil. Add cayenne pepper. Mix really well with a spoon. Line a small basket with a festive napkin and pile in pita bread. Serve beside the hummus.

● ● ● That's Sooo Cheesy ● ● ●

2 tablespoons (1/4 stick) of butter

1 8-ounce package of shredded Monterrey jack cheese

2 tablespoons of flour

1 1/2 cups of whole milk

1 bag o' tortilla chips

Melt butter in a medium-sauce pan over a low light. Slowly add cheese and stir with a wooden spoon until melted. Add flour and stir well until dissolved. Add 1/4 cup milk at a time, stirring constantly. Get it bubbling a bit, then transfer to a ceramic dip bowl. You can garnish with chopped tomatoes, scallions, salsa, or sour cream.

● ● ● Dance Mix ● ● ●

1/2 cup of raisins or dried cranberries

1/2 cup of peanuts or cashews

1/2 cup of sunflower seeds

1/2 cup of cheese puffs

1/2 cup of mini pretzels

1/2 cup of M&Ms

Start with a big Ziplock bag. Drop in each of the ingredients. Seal and shake well. Pour into three cereal-sized bowls and place on tables around the dance floor.

● ● ● Wildwings ● ● ●

3 pounds of plain precooked chicken wings

1 16-ounce jar of apricot preserves

1 package of taco seasoning

1 stick of unsalted butter

1/2 cup of ketchup

Warm up chicken wings in the oven. Empty preserves, seasoning, and ketchup into a medium-sized sauce pan. Simmer on low until melted and well combined. Transfer warm wings to a large dish. Pour sauce over wings and stir until well coated. Place on a serving tray. Celery sticks and blue cheese dressing make good company.

Have LOTS of napkins handy!

● ● ● Sweet Balls o' Fire ● ● ●

1 pound of precooked meatballs

1 32-ounce jar of grape jelly

1 12-ounce jar of chili sauce

1 8-ounce can of crushed pineapple

Empty chili sauce, crushed pineapple, and grape jelly into a medium-sized sauce pan. Simmer on low until melted and well combined. Add precooked meatballs. Cover. Simmer until hot, hot, hot. Transfer into a cool serving dish. Poke several of the meatballs with plastic swords, and put extras on the side.

● ● ● Pizza from the Pizanos ● ● ●

1 phone number for local pizza parlor

Enough money for pizza

Lots of hungry guests

Dial the phone. Say, "I'd like to have an order delivered," and give them your info. Get enough pizza for 2–3 slices per guest if that's the only dinner food you're serving. Ask how much it's gonna be. Make sure you have enough $ for the pizza and a tip for the delivery guy (or girl).

● ● ● Skew-Ups ● ● ●

1 package of 6-inch wooden skewers

2 cups of pineapple chunks (save the juice)

2 cups of large seedless grapes

2 cups of green apple chunks

2 cups of orange segments

2 cups of melon chunks

2 cups of banana slices

1 jar of maraschino cherries

Combine cherry juice and pineapple juice in a small bowl. Skewer and alternate the fruit. When finished, place the skewers on a baking sheet and pour pineapple/cherry juice mixture on top, making sure to coat the banana. Place skewers in a big enough bowl so that they don't topple over the sides.

● ● ● Chewy Chocolate Chip Cookies ● ● ●

1 package of chocolate-chip morsels
(Be sure to get the ones with the recipe on the back!)

Whether you go with the "from scratch" version (which we totally recommend for a great time) or slice off the "log," follow the package directions for hot, gooey treats. Makes the house smell great too!

● ● ● MYOS* ● ● ●

* MAKE YOUR OWN SUNDAE

Tub of chocolate ice cream	2 cans whipped cream
Tub of vanilla ice cream	1 jar maraschino cherries
Tub of strawberry ice cream	Lots of colored sprinkles
1 jar of fudge topping	1 jar of fruit topping

Jar of butterscotch topping

Jar of wet nuts (if you like wet nuts—we don't)

Maybe some M&Ms, chocolate chips, Reeses Pieces or other peanutty-chocolately candy, gummy bears, you get the idea . . .

You don't need directions for this. Just go all out!

It's better to have a little too much food than not enough.

BUT TRY TO SAVE as much as you can. Pack up leftovers and store in the fridge.

pets@parties.what2do/

Some **dogs** and **cats** and even some **birds** are really social. They just love being around people. But others might not like **people** at all. If you have a pet, there are some things to **think** about:

If you have a "peanut pet" like **Pico** (see page 58), and there are lots of people in your house, you should be **careful** that he or she doesn't get stepped on or sat on. (With really small pets, like **toy dogs** or **kittens**, it *could* happen.) Or if you have an older dog who's a bit grouchy, he or she might snap at (or even bite) one of your **guests**. That would be bad. This could happen even if your dog is young and **healthy**. Remember that there's *always* a chance an animal might do something **unexpected** when we least expect it.

Let your guests know what pets you have before they arrive. This way, if there's any reason they can't be around **animals**, such as a **fear** of dogs or bad **allergies**, they can decide not to come or just stay a short time. If there's anything guests need to know about your pet, tell them beforehand, such as Iago *will* **bite** your finger if you stick it in his face, or whatever else you know may annoy your pet and cause a bad **response**.

During the party, your pet needs to be able to get away from the **crowd**, like in a bedroom or somewhere else he or she feels **comfortable**, like a crate if you have a dog. Cats can usually find a place behind a couch or **under a bed**.

Pico is my Chihuahua. He's so little, so I usually carry him around for the first part of the party. Everyone wants to hold him, and he's usually okay with it. But eventually I'll put him in his crate so he doesn't become overwhelmed by all the hugs and kisses.   —Jayne

Iago is my African grey parrot. He's more like my brother than a pet. My parents adopted him after I was born, and we've pretty much grown up together. When I have my friends over for poker night (we play for chips, not $), Iago sits on his perch and joins in the conversation. He laughs when we laugh and answers our questions, usually w/ a loud, screeching "No"! Yeah, he's really smart, but he's got a lot to learn about poker.   —Jon

If you know your pet isn't friendly, make plans for him or her to be some place else while the party is going on. Also, don't allow anyone to tease your pet and make sure that any-one who handles your pet knows what they're doing. If your pet is around for the party, you or a trust-ed friend should keep an eye on him or her.

If you're at a party where there are furry, feathery, or scaly creatures, ask the party thrower if it's ok to interact w/ them.

OH NO, PANDEMONIUM!

SCENARIO #1 You invite 15 people but 40 show up! (Who are they & where the **heck** did they **come** from?)

SCENARIO #2 Someone brings a keg of **beer**. (How did they get it anyway?)

SCENARIO #3 2 of your guests **disappear** & you find them in your parents' bedroom. (**Ewwww!**)

SCENARIO #4 A bunch of people are **smoking** pot in your backyard. (Bad idea!)

SCENARIO #5 Someone **breaks** your mom's favorite vase. (That's gonna **cost** you.)

SCENARIO #6 Your **neighbors** call the cops cause the music's "**too loud.**" (Probably is.)

What's the common **denominator** in all these scenarios? Probably that your parents aren't home or are out of town. So you made the **decision** to have a party while your parents were gone, or maybe they even gave you **permission**. Who knows? What you do know is that the party is out of **control**, and you've gotta do something, **quick**:

- Turn off the music, and turn on all the lights.

- Gather your good friends and ask them to help you spread the word that the party's over.

- Tell the keggers and stoners to take their "stuff" and go.

- Tell your guests to get out of your parents' bedroom.

- Pick up the broken pieces and start thinking about how you're gonna pay for that.

- Hope that nothing valuable's missing.

- Tell the cops the party's breaking up, and be respectful.

- Clean up as best as you can, and come clean w/ your parents when they get back.

- Follow the rules for Keeping Your Party *Your* Party the next time you have a party.

Keeping Your Party *Your* Party

Rule #1 Don't let anyone in who you didn't invite (unless someone checked w/ you first).

Rule #2 Keep the party in one room, like a finished basement or den. Let your guests know that bedrooms are off limits.

Rule #3 After all your guests arrive, lock the front and back doors. (You don't want people just walking in uninvited.)

Rule #4 Put away any valuables and breakables before the party starts.

Rule #5 Enjoy the music but don't blast it so that it can be heard outside.

Rule #6 Have a set time for the party to end. You don't have to throw people out at that time, but start winding things down.

JacoB's

story

Party "Issues"

Parties are a great chance to hang out with friends and maybe meet new people. It's a great atmosphere, so you really can't help but feel happy. Everyone's laughing, dancing, singing, eating, and talking. But there are some issues to avoid to keep it that way.

Parents are an important factor. If a party is happening because there are no parents around, dead doesn't begin to describe what'll happen if you get caught. If you're a guest and the parent walks into a hall crowded with kids, you've really only got two options: run or stay. Run means you're bailing on your friend (and you will be in worse trouble if you do get caught). Stay means you will definitely get in trouble, but it does mean you didn't ditch your friend. So, really, the choice is up to you, but it's a much better idea to avoid that situation in the first place by checking beforehand to see if the parent knows. If you are the one having the party, you're better off letting your parents know what you're planning.

Fights would be the next obvious issue to consider. If you're the host, try not to have two or more people there who are prone to fighting. You don't want to have to play peacemaker. Fights generally don't happen, but when they do, it's disastrous. Something small will happen, maybe one kid bumped into another and they didn't like each other, but someone will throw a punch, and it all goes downhill from there. Stay out of the fight, and don't encourage it.

The last major issue is substance abuse (drugs and/or alcohol). I've never been to a party where that's been an issue before because the people I hang out with tend to be straight edge, but I personally think it's one of the worst things that can happen at a party. Sometimes it's just one person who makes an idiot out of himself by drinking or doing drugs (if this sounds like you, you're building a massive problem for yourself, so stop before you get in too deep). Other times, it's a whole group of people who end up wrecking the house or worse.

Other than that, parties are great whether you are the host or guest. As long as you watch out for yourself and your friends and make sure nothing is going on around you that's bad, you'll be fine and you'll have a great time.

Jacob C.

Jacob's right. These three issues are key in determining if the party is headed in the right direction. If a parent is unaware that a party is taking place that usually means that other things might be happening too that probably shouldn't be. "Watch out for yourself and your friends" is good advice. Thanks, Jacob. We totally recommend it.

Will there be **dancing** at your party or at the party you're going to? There usually is at big parties, with a dance floor and a **DJ** or **band**, sometimes even **dancers**. But it doesn't have to be a formal **party** for there to be dancing.

Some of us just seem to have natural **rhythm** and can dance to just about **anything** (sometimes anywhere). But that doesn't mean everyone does. What about **you**?

- Do you like to dance? **Cool.**

- Do you not like to dance? **That's ok.**

- Do you wish you could dance but you feel awkward and uncoordinated? **That's tough.**

RHythM

We think dancing is lots of **fun** and sometimes don't get why some people just don't like or want to do it. But **talking** w/ people like Jule helps us get it a little better. Here's what she says:

> **"**Whenever I go to parties, everyone starts dancing, but I just don't feel the rhythm, and I hate it when my friends try to drag me on to the dance floor—it's so embarrassing. I'm always making excuses when people ask me why I'm not dancing, like I hurt my ankle or something.**"**

Thinking up **excuses** takes a lot of Jule's energy and gets in the way of her **fun**. Maybe being **honest** would be better, like saying, "No thanks, I don't want to dance" or even "Thanks, but I have **two left feet!**" and making a joke out of it.

Everyone has different **talents** and dancing might not be your thing. But if you really want to dance but just don't feel **comfortable**, you'll need a bit of **courage** to get your body moving along w/ everyone else's. Try to determine what the problem is. Is it really that you *can't* dance or that you're just **afraid** to dance in front of people because they might **judge** you?

Think about this: when there's a **crowded** dance floor and people are doing all sorts of **crazy** moves, no one's really paying attention to what you're doing. And **anyone** who is paying attention to how you look out there probably isn't on the dance floor themselves, so **who** are they to say anything?

If you **truly** don't want to dance, that's totally your business. **Dancing** shouldn't be something to stress about. **Steer clear** of the dance floor if you really don't want someone to **pull you in**. And If you're one of the dancers who tries to drag your **awkward** friend out on the dance floor, give him or her a **break** and just do your own thing.

If dancing is **important** to you, but you just don't feel comfortable, consider taking **lessons**.

BLAST from the Past

"Shout" is one of the top party songs of all time. If you've ever been on the dance floor at a wedding, you've probably thrown your arms in the air w/ all the "old-timers."

Released in 1959, "Shout" is almost 50 years old! It's a song we can dance to with our grandparents, our parents, and our friends. Now that's something to shout about!

We bet you've got a **conundrum**—virtually all of us do. What's that? A *conundrum* is a **problem** that usually has a **complex** answer. We could've called it "Problems and Solutions," but we think *conundrum* is cooler.

If you've got a conundrum, go to jonandjayne.com and click on CONUNDRUMS & SOLUTIONS. We'll put our heads 2gether and try to help you (and other people who have the same problem) out w/ our "**solution**" in an upcoming issue.

We'll also check w/ **Dr. Toni** (see her bio on page 116) to be sure we're on the right track. Dr. Toni's pretty **cool** and always has some good stuff to say.

But don't wait for us! If you've got a **serious** problem, talk to an **adult** you trust. Don't let your conundrum get the best of you. Find a **solution**!

Conundrums & Solutions

Conundrum

I'm having a party, and I sent out invitations to everyone on my list. Then, two of my best friends had a big fight and now they told me that they won't come to my party if the other one is there. How do I decide between them?

Erin

Solution

Don't do anything right away. Give your friends some time to cool off. There's a chance they will work out their problem before the party. A good friend really wouldn't expect you to choose.

Dr. Toni Says:

Definitely do not "uninvite" anyone . . . that's just not fair. At the same time, let both of them know they are important to you and that you really would like each of them to attend. **DO NOT** get pulled into talking negatively to one friend about the other. Express concern for their feelings and be supportive. Say something like, "I know it will be weird if you're still not talking, but I really want you both to be there—maybe you can just avoid each other for now." Confronting their angry or hurt feelings at the party is not a good idea, so suggest that they just keep out of each other's way for the night. Of course, advising them to try to work out their problems, either before or after the party, *is* a good idea. And being a mutual friend, you can help with that.

Conundrum

I have different groups of friends (some from summer vacation, some from band, and some from my neighborhood). I don't think these groups really "get" each other, and I'm sort of like a different person with each group. Do I have a small party and just invite one group, or do I have a bigger party and take my chances?

Michael

Solution

Having different groups of friends can make for a more interesting mix. At most parties, you'll see people hanging out in different groups, even if they're from the same place. After a while, when they feel more comfortable, they'll go in search of others. Maybe one of your "summer" friends plays an instrument or has similar interests to your "neighborhood" friend.

Introduce friends from one group to friends in another—you may be surprised at how well they'll get along. Give them a chance to get to know each other. Remember, they all have at least one thing in common: YOU!

 Dr. Toni Says:

It completely depends on what kind of a party you want to have. If your objective is to have a big bash where people just sort of hang out, dance, and get to know one another, then it's fine to mix groups. Of course, it may be more work for you to make introductions and divide your time among a bunch of different groups. Jon and Jayne are right: you'd be surprised—people have more in common than you'd think, and new friendships could be formed. If you want a smaller, more intimate party, then just invite friends from one of the groups. This will allow for more of a bonding experience, where you can get to know each other really well and develop deeper connections.

CoNUNdrUM

Whenever I go to a party, I end up by myself on a couch in some corner. I feel awkward, but I don't know how to get into conversations or be "part of the group." Just walking to the door makes me nervous, and I wonder what people think of me. How can I be more at ease in situations like this?

Leon

SoLUtioN

If you always find yourself on a couch in the corner, avoid couches and corners. In this issue, we talk about having a "party partner," someone you know or trust to hang with you during the party. Find out who else is going and talk to them beforehand about keeping you in the mix.

If all else fails, just turn to the person who's sitting on the couch next to you and say hello.

Dr. Toni Says:

Social anxiety, or fear of situations where you're expected to interact with people, is common. Here are three steps for confronting such fears: First, try to think in positive ways. Write down the things about you that are fun and interesting. Remember these things when you are going to the party (saying, "I'm funny," "I'm good at sports," or "I'm creative," for example). Tell yourself that you will have fun, that you're a good person, and that people will like you once they get to know you.

Next, prepare. Rehearse some lines or think about some subjects to talk to other guests about. Imagine yourself talking to people, laughing, and having fun. Then, when you are actually there, push through your fears, walk up to someone who looks approachable, and say hello. This is my **be afraid but do it anyway** strategy. Don't let the fear keep you from doing something. Ask open-ended questions so that you can rely more on listening, rather than on talking, until you are more comfortable jumping in with your own thoughts and stories.

BYOB*

When you throw a party, you're the one who sets the rules. **It's all you!** You decide who you're gonna invite and what you're gonna serve. You make plans for the entertainment, set the mood w/ **music** and lighting, and hope all your **efforts** are worth it.

Parties usually take on a life of their own, but if you've done a good job setting the **stage**, your party should be a **huge success**!

We **think** the most important party decision you can make is to **not** serve alcohol (or allow some **moron** to sneak it in). But when it comes to alcohol (and drugs), not everyone makes the right

*BRING YOUR OWN BRAIN

decision. That's why you might find yourself at a party where alcohol is being served (either out in the open or **undercover**), and this is when you **need** to use your head, like Bridget:

> "I was dating this guy Sam for like two weeks over the summer when I was staying at my dad's. He invited me to a party and my dad was like 'Sure, go.' So I went. It was in his friend's basement. There were about 15 people, and they were friendly mostly. The girl whose house it was asked me if I wanted a beer. I said 'No, thanks, I don't drink.' She shrugged and said that was cool and handed a beer to Sam. He took it. I didn't say anything. Nobody got stupid drunk while I was there, but when it was almost 11 (my curfew), Sam was on his third beer. I had a few choices: I could walk the 15 blocks to my dad's, get in the car with Sam, or call my dad and ask him to pick me up. I called a taxi instead and was home at exactly 11."

Bridget made a **smart** choice. It's a good idea to have the number for a taxi or car service w/ you when you go out. Walking the streets **alone** at night wasn't a good option. Bridget was also **worried** that her dad would be angry if she called for a ride. Considering the **choices**, lots of parents will **agree** to pick up their kids with no Qs asked (until the next day).

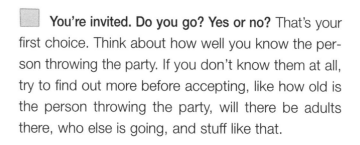

SHOULD YOUR BRAIN . . .
✓ Accept or ✗ Decline?

☐ **You're invited. Do you go? Yes or no?** That's your first choice. Think about how well you know the person throwing the party. If you don't know them at all, try to find out more before accepting, like how old is the person throwing the party, will there be adults there, who else is going, and stuff like that.

☐ **Will there be alcohol* or drugs at the party?** If the answer is "Yes," take a raincheck. Ultimately, you're the one who's gonna decide whether or not to go, but you really need to carefully consider the potential dangers of going to a party where there will be temptations and pressure.

☐ **Do you have a "party partner"?** Someone, or a few people, you can rely on who will be going to the party too? (It's great to socialize w/ lots of different people, but you should always keep your party partner in your line of sight as much as possible.) No one like that, or no one you really trust? We say, "Decline."

Parties that also include adults, like formal celebrations, usually have a bar for people over 21. We're not talking about those kinds of parties.

☐ **Are you going to join the crowd** if there ends up being alcohol or drugs at the party? (We hope not!) This is a decision you need to make before you accept the invite, even if you are pretty sure there won't be anything like that going on. And stick to your decision—even under pressure.

☐ **Do you have a way to get home?** Make arrangements before the party, and have a backup plan. Don't get stranded and **TOTALLY NEVER** get in the car w/ anyone who's been doing drugs or alcohol—even if they insist they're fine, cause they're not. Have access to a phone (a cell phone is best) so you can call for car service or call home for someone to pick up. Even if a friend plans to do the driving, make sure someone else will be available to pick you up if necessary. Are you doing the driving? Make sure your answer to the question above is an **ABSOLUTE NO**.

DR. TONI TELLS THE SPINE-TINGLING TRUTH ABOUT DRUGS & ALCOHOL

Here's the way I see it: Ultimately, you're going to make up your own mind about whether or not to do illegal drugs or drink alcohol . . . but before you do, you should know what could happen.

Before we get to the facts, I have some important questions to ask you, the most important being:

WHAT'S WRONG WITH YOUR MIND THAT YOU WANT TO CHANGE IT?

Maybe you just need to learn to **feel better** about yourself and become more **outgoing** and **friendly**, or less **overpowering**. Before you take such a big risk like doing drugs or drinking alcohol, ask yourself these questions and **consider** the **consequences**:

▼ Do you really want to let a pill, powder, or glass of liquid control you and your actions? Think about what could happen if YOU were not in control of yourself. Scary, right?

▼ Are you willing to get into a car with someone who is in really bad shape and may end up wrapping the car around a tree? Happens quite often, unfortunately. How would you feel if YOU were that driver?

▼ Are you willing to give up your fun and your freedom because you carelessly had sex while under the influence and now you're going to be a parent? Think carefully about this one: How would you feel about raising a child, dealing with an abortion, or putting your baby up for adoption?

Okay, if you've answered all of these questions and **STILL** want to drink alcohol or take drugs, read on.

THE FACTS

● ALCOHOL

It's a depressant. It slows the central nervous system and blocks messages meant for the brain. This affects judgment and the ability to keep yourself from doing something dangerous, life-changing, or just really embarrassing. Alcohol can also impair your ability to reason or learn and affects short-term memory.

It's not always fun when you drink. And it's illegal before you're 21. So, be smart and take it seriously.

● NICOTINE

Nicotine is a drug that is in tobacco leaves, and it's HIGHLY addictive. When you smoke, you inhale about 1 to 2 milligrams at a time . . . just enough to keep you smoking. A drop of pure nicotine can kill a person. The tar that's in cigarettes increases the risk of diseases such as lung cancer and emphysema.

Didn't you see that commercial with the guy who had a hole in his throat from smoking?

The risks are just too obvious. Smoking can become a lifelong habit. And besides, your breath and clothes will smell really, really bad.

I did. Totally YUCK!

● MARIJUANA (POT, GRASS, WEED, REEFER)

Marijuana is the name for a plant—the hemp plant—that, alone, doesn't seem so harmful. People say getting "high" feels good and can make you feel giddy or relaxed. Cool, right? Think again. Pot's active ingredient is tetrahydrocannabinol (THC). THC can slow your reaction time, affect your judgment, and lead to trouble with learning and memory. The memory loss can, in fact, be permanent. If you play sports, do gymnastics, or dance, your coordination can be impaired. And, like cigarettes, smoking it can cause lung cancer.

So you wanna laugh? Put on an episode of Family Guy instead. Wanna relax? Take yoga or just chill with your friends.

● ECSTASY OR "X"

It's a stimulant and a hallucinogen. That means that it will rev you up and can make you see and/or hear things that aren't real. Ecstasy is popular at *raves* (all-night dance parties). It seems really cool and hip to be part of it . . . N O T! Sure, you dance for hours, but you can also become anxious and agitated. Many people feel dizzy or get the chills; some may even

FREAK OUT. Ecstasy is made in secret "labs" and all kinds of impure stuff may be added to it—it's definitely not safe. This is an easy one: DON'T DO IT.

By all means, dance . . . but when you get tired, go home and go to sleep!

● COCAINE (COKE, BLOW, SNOW)
CRACK ("SMOKABLE" COKE)

Cocaine is an extremely addictive stimulant. No joke, don't even try it—cause you'll likely want to try it again . . . and then it's bad news from there. Goodbye money, goodbye friends, goodbye health, goodbye future. Coke can cause heart attacks, breathing problems, strokes, and seizures. It can make you do violent things and get you into a whole lot of trouble.

There's nothing cool about cocaine. Period. Want a buzz? Try an espresso.

● HEROIN (SMACK, JUNK)

Heroin is an opium-containing drug processed from morphine (a narcotic), which is derived from poppy plants. Then it's "cut" (diluted) with all kinds of other substances—which is why you never know how strong it'll be. Which is why people overdose and **DIE**. Which is why you'd be CRAZY to even try it. The initial feeling of euphoria is followed by extreme drowsiness and mental cloudiness. In other words, you'll be completely unable to function. And then you'll want more. Cause, like cocaine, it's highly addictive. And the vicious cycle continues.

Heroin destroys lives and kills. Enough said.

● INHALANTS (WHIPPETS, POPPERS)

These are chemical vapors (in household products) that are breathed in, producing mind-altering effects. Like alcohol, they make you feel intoxicated or high and cause slurred speech and dizziness . . . but this lasts only about two minutes. Long-term use can result in damage to the nervous system and cause muscle spasms and tremors, memory problems, and harm to vital organs. Inhale too much at once and you can lose consciousness and even die.

There's too much that can go wrong with inhalants. Don't risk it.

● LSD (ACID)

LSD is a mood-altering psychedelic chemical that is unpredictable and can cause delusions and hallucinations. In other words, it alters the way your brain works and distorts your perception of reality. It can raise your body temperature, heart rate, and blood pressure, and cause sleeplessness and loss of appetite. It may also cause rapid, intense emotional swings. The effects can last for six to twelve hours, so if you're having a "bad trip," it will be a long ride.

Do you really want to feel like a schizophrenic?

I hope you realize that if you decide to do drugs even after knowing that the effects can be **DEADLY**, you should seek professional help. None of the problems we face in life can be made better with illegal drugs. *Always consider the consequences— and please don't do it.*

CarLLa'S

t o r y

Stupid Drunk

About a year ago I was pressured into going to a party that I really didn't want to go to by my friend Stephanie. At first I had fun dancing and flirting, just an average teenage party. That's what I thought. Since this was my first "real high school party," I was having fun. Everything was perfect, right? I had my parents' trust and no curfew.

Just perfect? Not really. About an hour after the party had started, these guys (I don't know who they were) walked in with lots of beer and hard liquor. I went over to my friend Stephanie and asked her if we could go home. She told me to relax and that we'd leave after she had a beer. So I stayed and waited. After she finished her beer, I asked her again. She told me to stop being a buzz kill. She then grabbed another beer, then another, and another, till she couldn't even stand up straight.

We started arguing, and she grabbed her keys to go. I tried to take her keys away from her even though I didn't drive yet, but she pushed me away and disappeared somewhere. I didn't think she'd leave without me, but pretty soon I realized she had abandoned me at the party. So I had to call my parents for a ride home, which was totally embarrassing, but better than endangering my life by getting into a car with a drunken party-goer.

The next day, I found out that Stephanie got into a car crash. She passed away. I wish I could have tried a little harder to stop her. But I realized I could have died, too, if I had gone along with her. Luckily, I didn't lose my life. But I did lose a friend.

Carlla S.

All kinds of things can happen when everybody gets together for a party and some of it is just not good. We each need to be responsible for ourselves. We should look out for our friends, but we can't take responsibility for their actions.

We never go driving with anyone who's under the influence of anything. We think a little embarrassment from having to call your parents is totally worth your life. And since a lot of our friends are too young to drive anyway, we usually make arrangements for a ride before going.

We feel it's better to say good-bye if there is anything at the party we'd rather avoid. If you can't have a good party without serving or drinking alcohol (or worse), then it's probably not a good party to begin with.

Danny's Story

Completely Sober

There have been lots of fatal drunk-driving
accidents in my area with teenagers behind the
wheel coming back from parties and celebrations,
so a community group in my area decided to
throw a party as part of a town effort to stop
drunk driving. A lot of parties get passed up
simply because they're "dry," but some of the
best times I've ever had were completely sober.
So, when a few of my friends volunteered to
throw the party for the community group, I told
my friends I'd help them set up. It took us all
afternoon to get everything arranged at the town
theater (where the party was), and to tell you the

truth, I REALLY thought it was going to be lame, but I stuck around anyway. I had been thinking about going to some other pretty huge parties across town, but I didn't want to end up stuck somewhere without a ride later.

As it turned out, some wealthy people from our community donated eight grand in prizes to the party to try and get kids (like myself) to go. There was a whole bunch of stuff that would be raffled off as the night went on. I figured I'd stick around, put my name in a few of the buckets, and just see what happened. I ended up watching a pretty sick Ska band play a couple of songs, then talking with the guitarist for a while about guitars (which I'm fanatical about!).

After that, I ended up just wandering around talking to everybody, and I met some really interesting people and other people I already knew. There was a thirty-person Twister mat, a pair of DDR2 machines, Ping-Pong, karaoke, and a whole bunch of other stuff that we'd set up. The best part about everything was that it was all free (and I was very broke).

When the party started to wind down, the theater put on a movie for the people who decided to stick around to watch and then gave away the remaining prizes.

It was getting late (like 4 a.m. late). I was supertired, but luckily there was lots of coffee, and I still had my name in for a couple of things that hadn't been given away yet. Long story short, I ended up winning a laptop, got to have a good time chilling with some familiar faces, didn't have to worry about finding a designated driver (total bummer at 4 in the morning), and didn't wake up the next day with a hangover.

In the end, I went home with more than a caffeine buzz (and a new computer): I learned that people make the fun, not what they drink.

Dan W.

Dan was lucky—he found a fun party where nobody had to get crunk to enjoy it. That's the kind of party we like: fun, games, and nobody throwing up or crashing their car.

You may not think it's ideal to have adults at a party, but chances are it won't get out of hand either. Look for school or community sponsored parties in your area and go with your friends. After all, it's the people who make the party happen.

"Thanks, But NO Thanks"

NO is possibly one of the most **important** words in our vocabulary. It can keep us from making **mistakes** and getting into **trouble**.

If there's a group of people **pushing** you to do something you don't **want** to do or if you simply feel **pressured** to do something cause everybody else is doing it, think about the potential **consequences** of participating. Don't just throw CAUTION to the wind. There's a good **chance** it'll ricochet and hit you in the back of the head and knock you out cold and flat. So remember that word—it's the keyword: "**consequences**."

Get out of where you are if you have to—**remove** yourself from the situation. In other words, leave. Whatever you do, don't allow other people to make important **decisions** for you.

When you stand firm, people should **respect** you for your **decisions**. If they don't, that's okay, cause the most important **person** *will* respect you for making the right decision—and that's **you**.

Sometimes you might end up the **only** person in the crowd not doing something that you don't think is **cool,** and you might feel like an awkward outsider. That feeling won't last **forever,** so be **proud** of yourself for being your own person!

How to Say No . . .

For the really clueless among us:

1 Place the tip of your tongue on the roof of your mouth behind your front teeth.

2 Begin to engage your vocal cords.

3 Form an "N" sound as you allow your tongue to drop to it's natural position.

4 Immediately begin to make an "O" sound as you form your lips into a small circle.

5 Disengage your vocal cords.

Practice these 5 steps often. Try it whenever you are faced with something you really don't want to do (or know you really shouldn't do). Try firm NO's and soft NO's, but make it count every time you say it.

If someone doesn't like the way you say NO or the fact that you are saying it, that's their problem, not yours. You're in charge of who and what you say NO to.

QUICKIE

Gotta love a **quiz**! This issue's **Quickie** has 10 mostly party-related Qs from QuizMaster Anthony P. See if u know the answers. If u don't, **Google** it. Then go to **jonandjayne.com** to see if you're right. Click on **"QUICKIES."** The password is **PARTYON**. Catch the "Fresh Factoids" for each answer.

#1 How many colors are used for the dots in the classic party game Twister?

#2 In the 2007 musical *Hairspray*, where do Tracy Turnblad and her friends go to dance at a "platter party"?

#3 What potentially dangerous activity happens at a "rainbow party"?

4
Which young star was "transformed" into Harrison Ford's young sidekick for the 2008 movie *Indiana Jones & the Kingdom of the Crystal Skull*?

5
What color dress should a young woman wear to her own debutante ball?

6
If you are giving a Goth party, what color should your candles be?

7
What spooky device, sometimes used at parties, has participants asking questions of the "spirits"?

8
How many color-coded frets are there on the guitar console used for Wii's "Guitar Hero III"?

9
After "partying," where do "Harold and Kumar" go for some burgers in their 2004 movie?

10
Which "colorful" singer-songwriter hit it big in 2001 with the popular single "Get the Party Started"?

AUTHORITY

When it comes to **throwing** and **going** to parties, what do we do when what we want **conflicts** with what our parents want? It's a tough call. Let's look at the following **sticky** situations.

Sammy says:

❝There's going to be a really big party next weekend and all my friends are going, but my parents said I can't go to any party that's not being supervised by adults.❞

SECRET: Sammy's going to tell his parents that he's staying over his friend's house, but then go to the party instead.

97

Jackie says:

> **❝**I want to throw a party for all my friends but my parents don't want some wild bash happening at their house.**❞**

SECRET: Jackie is going to wait for her parents to go away for the weekend, then have everybody over.

Lots of people do stuff like this all the time, and lots of times they get away w/ it. . . . But sometimes they can get themselves into real **trouble**.

Before you do something your parents told you not to, **consider** why they said no. They're probably just looking out for your safety and not trying to make your life **tougher** than it already is.

Do you find it difficult to talk to your parents honestly about their **rules** and **expectations**? Have you tried explaining your point of view and reaching a **compromise** you can both live with? It's easier said than done, but it's worth a **chance** if you can get them to see things your way—or understand their point of view.

Let's see how it worked out for Sammy and Jackie:

Sammy went over to his friend's house and they went to the **party** together. The party turned out to be small and quiet. The guys had some snacks, **talked** with some people they met, and then hooked up with some **friends** and went over to the movie theater for an early show. They were back **home** before **curfew** and no one was the wiser. But Sammy still felt guilty about **lying** to his parents and wished he'd been able to talk with them about the **party**.

Jackie, on the other hand, told **everyone** about her party . . . and everyone came! Even though there was no alcohol or drugs evident at the party, some of the **guests** ended up making a **mess** of the house. Jackie spent most of the party **cleaning** up after her "guests" and **worrying** about stuff getting broken. Even **worse**, bad weather forced her parents to end their weekend **early** and they came **home** to find the house still a huge wreck.

While neither of these **scenarios** was as bad as some of the stories we've heard, there were no **happy** endings either. When we don't **agree** with our parents on the things we want to do, there are bound to be some **problems**. But there are ways to talk about what's bothering us and **vent** our **frustrations** without things coming to a head.

We keep **a lot** of personal stuff from our parents because if they knew everything about our **lives**, it would be really **awkward**. But we need to be able to share with them the important **stuff**, things that have the potential to **change** our lives.

If we just can't **talk** to our parents, it can **help** to talk to an older brother or sister, a **teacher**, a counselor, or a trusted **friend**—someone else who can give us advice . . . or just **listen**.

It's really not so bad having adult **chaperones** at parties. They don't have to **hang out** like part of the gang (that's usually not **cool**), but it's good for them to be available (or at least a phone call away) in case things get **sticky**.

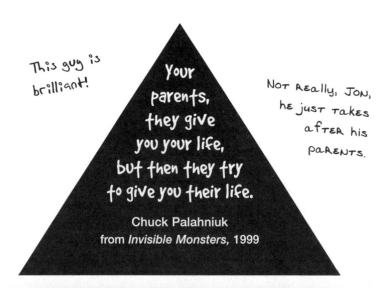

This guy is brilliant!

Your parents, they give you your life, but then they try to give you their life.

Chuck Palahniuk
from *Invisible Monsters*, 1999

Not really, Jon, he just takes after his parents.

ALex's

story

Alex's Next Top Model

It was almost New Year's Eve, and I wanted a cute, fun, and small New Year's Eve party. So I invited about 15 of my girlfriends. My only problem was that my parents were going to be home the whole night, and I was planning to be a little crazy and dance away!

Anyways as New Year's Eve was around the corner, my mom came up with a very cute idea for my party, which was to make it "Alex's Next Top Model." I told about five of my friends about my mom's idea, and they thought it was going to be lame. Meanwhile, my mom was more excited than

I was for this party, and I was having crazy thoughts about my friends not liking it. I was crushed.

It was eight o'clock and the party was just getting started. About 45 minutes passed, and my mom told all my friends to gather in the living room. So they did. As the words "Welcome to Alex's Next Top Model!" came out of her mouth, I knew I was in for trouble! But as the "contest" was continuing, it turned out that I was getting a kick out of it and so were my friends. Surprisingly, I think my mom felt like she was on of us! Anyways the contest was a blast, and I was loving every second of it. When the contest was about to end, no one quite wanted it to, but it definitely didn't mean we had to stop having fun.

The girl who won the contest got a gorgeous bracelet. Then we had pizza, snacks, and some sparkling grapejuice in champagne cups. It was really fun, because why get drunk when you're already having fun? It was about eleven o'clock and the ball was going to drop in an hour. The music was loud, and we all started dancing and taking pictures (pretending to be models to go with the theme) just like any other girl would do when they have fun. As midnight got closer, we all gathered around the TV, excited to see the ball drop. We counted the seconds like no others. As the ball dropped, we were all going crazy.

Some of the girls had to leave, but they left with a huge smile on their face and didn't really want to go. They all said is was the best party ever!! They all agreed that my mom is the best party planner ever with the best ideas and said they were expecting another outrageous party next year. Some of them stayed and slept over. We were up till about 2:30 a.m., playing games, laughing, and talking. I will never forget that New Year's Eve!

Alex G.

Alex (& her friends) had some doubts (we all probably would), but her mom came up with a really fun game. Hey, sometimes our parents can be cool—we just have to give them a chance (if we have to).

If you must have a chaperone at your party, come up with some activities you think your guests will enjoy and tell that person. This way your party will stay on track and you can still cut loose without things getting out of hand.

Krista's

story

Music, Food, and
NO PARENTS!

As long as you keep the basics of a party in mind,
and you have the right connections (know the
right people), you don't have to be popular to
have a good party. There aren't many things
you need for a rocking party, but you do need
these three basic things, which are TOTAL
NECESSITIES: music, food, and NO PARENTS!

We'll talk about the parent thing in a minute, but
first off, if you don't have any music, you might as
well not even throw a party. But don't go around
asking people what kind of music they like. I think

that would make you seem unsure and nervous. If you want to know what music to have, ask people to bring CDs or just mix genres up and have a big variety. Even if you have the money to hire a DJ, give him something to work with. If people will be dancing all night, they want good music.

During those dancing breaks, people want food to nibble on. I'm not saying that you should put a whole feast out like a chicken or ham. I suggest cheese platters and chips and dip. Maybe your parents could even make something for everyone to eat. Like I said, people will be dancing all night; usually they won't be vultures and attack all of the food after just one dance.

Now for the most important part: If your parents trust you enough and let you throw a party in the first place, you should really appreciate it. But the difficult part is yet to come. I don't think you or your guests would want your parents watching your every move when you just want to be free for the night. So, sit them down, talk to them, and discuss this issue and ask them to go out to dinner and enjoy themselves. Relax if they refuse, and talk to them about being cool about the "parents being there" issue. They don't have to stay away the whole night. You and your guests just want to be free to be yourselves, not to do anything bad, just to let go a little.

People rumor that only "known kids" in school can throw a good party. According to me, *everybody is anybody,* and people should be accepted for who they are. If you want to throw a party, follow my lead and remember my tip on what to always have: Music, Food, and NO PARENTS!

Krista T.

Krista's got some interesting ideas. She's so right about the music and food. The "no parents" thing is definitely something to consider when planning your party—and it's something to talk to your parents about . . . beforehand.

Krista had some good suggestions about how to talk w/ them to make your feelings on this clear.

Jon's update
...n Felicia's party

So me, Andy, and Pete went to Felicia's party. Pete's brother dropped us off around 8:45. The party was already OUT OF CONTROL. There were like 50 kids there, with more people showing up.

The front door was wide open, so we just went in. It was smoky and crazy and the music was BLASTING. We didn't even see Felicia. The only thing to drink was beer, and there was nothing to eat but the trail mix all over the carpet. So we stayed for like 10 minutes and then we left. We walked over to Andy's with some friends who we ran into at the party and checked out the new video game he got for his Wii.

At lunch on Monday, the rumors were all over the place. I don't even know how much of it was true, so I'm not even gonna repeat it—you can use your imagination.

What definitely happened is that the cops showed up at around 10 and broke up the party. Then they called Felicia's parents. Don't know what happened after that. I'm just glad my friends and I didn't stay . . . we all had a pretty cool time at Andy's.

JaynE SaYs 611: i wont say i told u so

JD GaTEr 110: ya right...think u just did

JaynE SaYs 611: ;)

JD GaTEr 110: so how was your date w/ whats his name

JaynE SaYs 611: i called him but he had other plans

JD GaTEr 110: good

JaynE SaYs 611: huh?

JD GaTEr 110: oh....I meant too bad

JaynE SaYs 611: hmmm. sure Jon

JD GaTEr 110: see ya 2 moro

JaynE SaYs 611: k. gnite

The Party's Over . . .

Whether you **throw** parties or **go to** parties, you'll definitely wanna **SURVIVE** them, especially if you wanna be around for our next issue.

You've probably got some **cleaning** up to do. When there's lots of people eating, drinking, dancing, playing games, and just having a **great time**, there's sure to be a **mess**. Hopefully, it's nothing a garbage bag or two can't hold!

It's ok if things don't go as **planned**—it's even ok if there was some **drama**. (There usually is.) And, yeah, there's a *chance* that stain from the Black Hole cocktail *might* come out of the new **carpet** in your family room with a professional cleaning. But in the end all that matters is that you were **true** to yourself.

Thanks for coming!

We hope you had a good time!

Get home safe!

What's the one thing you would wanna tell the whole world if you could?

We asked, and you answered.
Here's what some of you had to say. ⟶

Get heard, too. Go to jonandjayne.com,
click on "Tell the World!"
And then enter what you have to say.

Look for your message to the world
in an upcoming issue.

Tell the World

Peace and joy is the way to stay.
John Y.

Hey.
Felipe F.

Don't judge people by how they look, get to know them first. You won't regret it.
Ashley B.

Peace!!!
Kemely O.

Stop for a second and think about where you are now.
Ian B.

Live in peace.
David R.

Treat someone the way you would want to be treated.
Madison T.

Stay cool.
Jake H.

Why can't we be friends?
Lexi B.

Laugh more!
Carla C.

Be happy. =]
Samantha S.

Stop animal cruelty.
Anastasia C.

Just calm down.
Jason C.

Spend your time wisely. You can't take it back.
Brandon N.

Stop racism.
Steven S.

It's all about the hair.
Ryan P.

Save sharks, whales, and dolphins, please!
John R.

Surfing is the coolest sport ever!!!
Jenna J.

Live life to the fullest.
Sarah B.

Can't we just all get along? *Megan W.*

Don't let the little things in life bother you. The energy you use stressing about it can be put toward something useful.
Shaina K.

Don't be annoying and don't be stupid.
Tommy L.

You only live once.
Matthew C.

STOP LITTERING!
Shana H.

Just chill.
Matthew L.

Stop global warming.
Jennifer O.

You have a reason to live. Find it!
Alexandra M.

Open your mind (& ears) & shut your mouth.
Matt M.

Peace, Love, & Happiness.
Jessica G.

Live as much as you can.
Dylan W.

No Internet?!

That's OK. You can still be part of our **7F community**. To get the answers to the Quickie and the Drama, simply send a postcard to our publisher's place:

HCI Teens
3201 SW 15th Street
Deerfield Beach, FL 33442
Attention: Quickie & Drama Answers

CYA!

Thanks for hanging w/ us!
We hope you had fun and got something
out of our rantings and ramblings.
Hope you liked the stories from our
contributors. Got a story of your own?
We'd really like to hear from you,
so don't forget to visit us at
www.jonandjayne.com.
There's more to do & more to come.
Join our 7F community and get heard!

~Jon & Jayne

Meet the #2 Crew

Hello, we're **Carol** and **Gary R.**, and we make it possible for Jon and Jayne to get their word out. We live in mostly sunny Florida with our two dogs, one cat, one parrot, one iguana—and our son, **Justin**, who introduced us to Jon and Jayne.

My name is **Alex G.,** short for Alexandra. I'm 15 and a sophomore who loves to have fun. I enjoy playing sports and hanging out with my friends. One major thing I love is shopping! I love music—it's a beautiful thing. I believe music fills the empty parts of life and makes you feel better about yourself.

Hi, I'm **Alina B.** Live live in FL. I'm 16 years old and I'm a sophomore in high school. The one quote I live by is "Don't fear change, embrace it!" because, in a way, only good can come from it.

I'm **Ashley B.** I'm 15. I love to play softball, and I'm doing very well in school. I'm involved in the musical theatre program. I'm friends with people from all cliques, but I have more guy friends than girls because I find them easier to get along with. Some of my favorite things are Starbucks, friends, movies, music, concerts, chocolate, French fries, and surfing. Some of my least favorite things are spiders, liars, eggs, small spaces, and Spanish class.

Hi, my name is **Carlla S.** I'm 15 and a student in high school. I have a larger family so I learn many things from them. My sister sparked by passion for writing, and I'm glad I can share my experiences through something I enjoy. The best advice I can give is live for today, but do your best to not let today be your last day.

I'm **Dan W.** I'm 17. I enjoy playing guitar, drawing, and hanging out with my friends. I think everyone should write because it's an invaluable skill to have. Every good idea in history had to be written down at some point.

My name's is **Emily O**. I'm 16. I'm on varsity cross country, track, and basketball at my high school. I really like school and I'm very involved. I have a few different groups of friends and I love all of them. My favorite things to do are go to the beach, shop, and hang out with friends. I love making people happy. :)

Hi, I'm **Jacob C.** I'm navigating high school right now with as much finesse as I can manage. When I'm not there, my real life includes playing bass in a band, going geocaching with my dad and stepmother, hanging out with my friends, reading, and listening to music (I especially like the bands Bright Eyes and The Magnetic Fields).

Hi, my name is **John Y.**, but people call me **Mikey**. I am 13 years old. I'm on the soccer team. My best friends are Ashley, Brianna, & Dallas. I go online a lot, and I am always with my friends. I love to talk. I can't imagine being without music. I pay attention to the weather cause it concerns me.

Hi, I'm **Dr. Toni.** I'm a licensed psychologist practicing in New York, and I've worked directly with kids and teens since 1999 in community and school settings. My specialty is running groups for preteen and teenage girls. I currently have a private practice in New York.

Hey it's me, **Justin O.** I am about 5'10" and I love sports and being active. I'm a freshman in high school with a 3.3 grade point average. I also enjoy practicing karate. I have a junior black belt and an adult brown belt. Besides karate I also play football and basketball. All around, I'm a particularly athletic kid.

Hi, I'm **Kaitlyn R.** I'm 16. I loooove shopping, hanging out with my friends, and listening to music. I hate doing nothing. I think global warming is scary and that something has to be done about it. The things about school I dislike the most are homework and tests! They're so annoying.

Hi, readers, I'm **Krista T.** I have many friends and I'm the easiet person to get along with. My interests include music, art, and doing activities with my friends. Now that you know a little about me, I hope you can get a better picture of who I am.

I'm **Kristin R.** I'm 12 years old. I have two older sisters (who always make me laugh), a mom, a dad, and a puppy named Molly. I love to listen to music, chill with my friends, play computer games, and play with my dog. I kinda like shopping.

Hey, my name is **Max V.** I'm in the seventh grade and I'm 12 years old. My favorite things to do are chill, write, listen to music, play video games, and more chilling.

Hi, my name is **Megan R.** I'm 17. My favorite books are *After, Macbeth,* and *A Series of Unfortunate Events.* I also like to shop, listen to music, talk on the phone, and hang out with my friends.

Hey, I'm **Ryan ("Chili") P**. I'm 14, and I'm a black belt in American Kenpo. I just finished up co-leading a kenpo summer bootcamp for some of the younger students. I really enjoy teaching. I also like to skateboard, play guitar, go to the beach, and listen to music. I don't like shopping.

I'm **Samantha S.** I'm 14. I like music, movies, friends, and books. I talk to friends on myspace a lot. One of my favorite movies is *The Princess Bride* and one of my favorite books is *Harry Potter and the Prisoner of Azkaban.* My friends make me laugh, but sometimes they do really stupid things. I dislike mean people. I'm on the school debate and bowling teams.

My name is **Skylar H**. I recently turned 16 years old. I'm a black belt in Kenpo karate. I play on the basketball team at my school. My friends are an extremely important part of my life, and so is my family. I love to make people laugh. I enjoy watching teen drama movies about relationships, and reading books about the same kind of stuff. A big hobby of mine is working with children and making a difference in someone's life.

My name is **Wilson P.** and I'm currently a sophomore in high school. I wrote my story recently, but it happened when I was younger. I'm an outgoing person. I think family and friends are the most important aspects of my life.

Hello. I'm **Mindy H.**, and I'm in the party business. My company caters events like sweet sixteens, theme parties, weddings, and more in South Florida. On top of that, my husband and I run a school of self-defense. I have 2 teenage daughters and I am an advocate for children with the PTA. But with all I do, there's always time for a party, and if anyone can throw one, it's me.

This is **QuizMaster Anthony P**. I love movies and music and books and art and TV (especially Ernie Kovacs—look him up online!). I have worked in book publishing my entire career, including three years in children's books. I'm a happy stepdad to twins, which keeps life interesting.

ANY EXCUSE TO THROW A PARTY...

✔ School's out for the summer!

✔ It's Halloween, Christmas, Hannukah, Kwanza, New Year's, or whatever.

✔ It's your b-day or your friend's b-day.

✔ Your team just won the championship— or just played a good game.

✔ You just got great news!

✔ You just got bad news & need a pick-me-up.

✔ You or a friend is going away and u wanna have a last big bash.

Where Can I Find...?